The creative coloring in this book
is the work of:

_____

The Art of Coloring

Use markers, pens, pencils, crayons – any method you choose.
There is no right or wrong way.

Relax & enjoy your coloring experience!

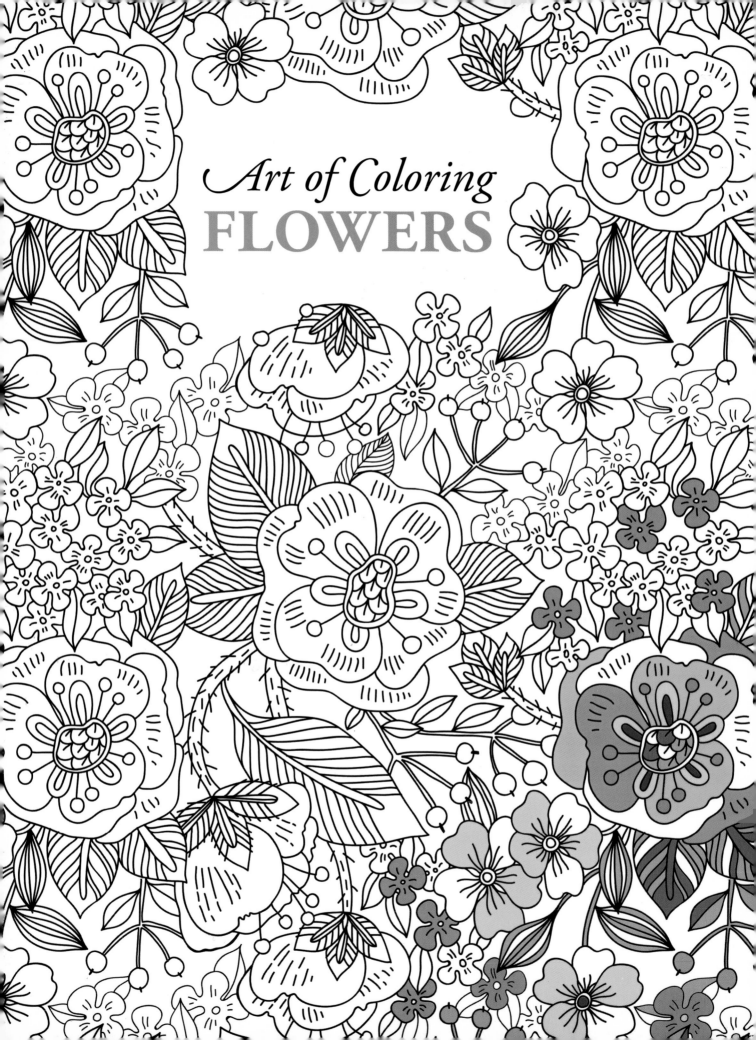

Art of Coloring
FLOWERS

Experiment to find the style you like best!

Markers Pencils Pens Crayons

Produced by Deckchair Press, an imprint of AE Publications Ltd., 60 Windsor Avenue, London, SW9 2RR, Tel. +44 1273 477374

All images supplied by AE Publications Ltd. / Shutterstock, Inc.

Compiled by: Jo Chapman
Publisher: Jonathan Grogan
Production Manager: Jim Bulley

Published by Leisure Arts, Inc., 104 Champs Blvd., STE 100, Maumelle, AR 72113-6738

Rediscover the calming benefits and creative stimulation of coloring! Effective for all ages, coloring has captured the imaginations of people around the world. Its meditative qualities benefit body and soul, to help you escape your worries and regain your concentration. Experience the magic of color therapy!

• 24 Designs on perforated sheets • Premium paper printed on one side only

ISBN-13: 978-1-4647-5454-8

50599

9 781464 754548

EAN

DECKCHAIR PRESS

LEISURE ARTS®
the art of everyday living
www.leisurearts.com

#6806 US $5.99/CAN $7.99

0 28906 06806 1

UPC

MADE IN U.S.A.